The Ethics Seminar Guide

Contemporary Ethical, Moral and
Responsibility Issues Based on Bible Stories

Kenneth E. Walsh

A companion booklet to
Bible Stories for All without the Dogma,
A Part of Cultural Literacy

Summit Crossroads Press
Columbia, MD 21045

Copyright 2020 © by Kenneth E. Walsh

All rights reserved, including the right to distribute, transmit, scan, copy, or reproduce any portion of this book.

No part of this book may be distributed, transmitted, scanned, copied, or reproduced without the author's permission, except you may reproduce the seminar questions and evaluation forms for use in an academic or congregational/church setting.

Send requests for permissions to kenwalsh3@icloud.com.

Discounted bulk orders for *The Ethics Seminar Guide*, and its companion book, *Bible Stories for All without the Dogma*, may be ordered directly by emailing your request to kenwalsh3@icloud.com. *The Teacher Supplement to Bible Stories for All without the Dogma* is available with bulks orders of the other books.

The 198-page teacher supplement contains reading comprehension questions, vocabulary development, essay writing, discussion questions, and assessment quizzes.

....

Direct quotes or quotes with minor modifications from the *Good News Bible, Today's English* ©American Bible Society, 1992, use the *Good News Translation*® (Today's English Version, Second Edition) © 1992 American Bible Society. All rights reserved.

Bible text from the *Good News Translation* (GNT) is not to be reproduced in copies or otherwise by any means except as permitted in writing by American Bible Society, 1865 Broadway, New York, NY 10023 (www.americanbible.org).

GNT

Library of Congress Control Number: 2020919909

ISBN: 978-0-9991565-9-9

Cover picture: Courtesy of pixabay.com.

In Praise of the Companion Book,
Bible Stories for All without the Dogma, A Part of Cultural Literacy

"An absolutely absorbing, engagingly articulate, impressively informative, expertly written, organized and presented study… is unique and an extraordinarily 'reader friendly' in tone, commentary, and style." *Midwest Book Review*

"…even among the nonreligious, one must have basic biblical literacy to fully understand Western society. Biblical references…abound in Western literature, art, and music... The bulk of Walsh's work walks readers through the major stories of the Old Testament in a straightforward, non-dogmatic way while providing brief historical and literary commentary for context. He also highlights important concepts and themes that run throughout the Old Testament that could be easily overlooked by those new to the Bible." *Kirkus Reviews*

"…presents all that it promises with unusual clarity and rich but not overwhelming context. The straightforward descriptions, thoughtful questions, and helpful panoramic views of human life in these regions and times should prove of great value to educators and facilitators, as well as anyone seeking intellectual support in their journeys of faith." Tara Hart, Ph.D.; Professor and Chair of Humanities; Howard Community College, Columbia, MD

"…richly informative text, aided by insights, notes, commentary and chapter references, aimed at helping believers and non-believers alike learn more fully about the Bible and its significant impact on our Western culture. It truly is a work worthy of engaging those who want to explore the place and influence of the Old Testament stories on the world we live in." Rev. Bill Watters, SJ, founder and past president of St. Ignatius Loyola Academy and Cristo Rey Jesuit High School, Baltimore, MD

"Allusions to Bible stories are ubiquitous in our American culture, and yet many of us are ignorant of the stories themselves. Walsh's dogma-free book is a welcome introduction to these time-tested stories that are relevant to persons of any faith or of none!" Rev. Paige Getty, Unitarian Universalist Congregation of Columbia, MD

"What a great, accessible resource for parents, students, and culturally curious adults alike, a most readable introduction to Old Testament stories, which continue to be a font of Western literature, culture, and values! ...filled with biblical excerpts, thoughtful notes, maps, and questions for reflection. Ken's Bible Stories is an indispensable reference for anyone curious about the Bible." Jeff Sindler, Head of School, Burgundy Farm Country Day School, Alexandria, VA

"…invites readers to engage with some of the foundational texts of Judaism and Christianity. Clear, inviting narrative, with helpful background information and thoughtful processing questions, helps us enter the worlds of such well-known biblical figures as Abraham and Sarah, Isaac, Jacob, Joseph, Moses, David, Solomon, and to understand why these stories have been shared for millennia." Gail Forsyth-Vail, retired Director of Lifespan Faith Engagement, Unitarian Universalist Association

ACKNOWLEDGEMENT

The Ethics Seminar Guide was written as a result of an encouraging discussion with John Ciccone, the President of St. Ignatius Loyola Academy, the middle school where I taught for 14 years. In the course of discussing my recently published book, Bible Stories for All without the Dogma, John mentioned that ethics was a topic of interest in many schools. From that discussion I developed the idea of a companion booklet to explore contemporary issues of ethics based on Bible stories.

In my Religion classes I used a seminar approach influenced by my readings and by two teacher workshops held by the Association of Independent Maryland Schools. While the seminars appeared to be easy to lead, I was surprised by the amount of effort I put into them - before, during, and after each seminar. I enjoyed doing it, and I was gratified by the student involvement and growth.

It is my hope that you will develop a better understanding of the Biblical stories and their influence on Western culture and explore the universal lessons that transcend the world's organized religions as you delve into contemporary ethical issues based on Bible stories.

Kenneth E. Walsh
September 28, 2020

TABLE OF CONTENTS

Background 1
Introduction 3
The Seminar Process 4
The Real World 9
Socrates 10
Student's Seminar Evaluation 13
Students' Whole Class Seminar Evaluation 14
The Main Parts of the Bible 15
Seminar 1. Adam and Eve 16
Seminar 2: Cain and Abel 17
Seminar 3: Noah 18
Seminar 4: Abraham & Egypt 19
Seminar 5: Abraham & the Travelers 20
Seminar 6: Abraham, Hagar, & Ishmael 21
Seminar 7: Abraham & Isaac 22
Seminar 8: Jacob & Easau: Sibling Rivalry 25
Seminar 9: Jacob's Deception of His Father, Isaac 24
Seminar 10: Laban Deceives Jacob! 25
Seminar 11: Jacob & Esau Reconciliation 27
Seminar 12: Joseph, the Favorite Son & Annoying Brother 28
Seminar 13: Joseph Is Enslaved and Then Unfairly Imprisoned 29
Seminar 14: Joseph Gives God Credit for His Ability to Interpret Dreams 30
Seminar 15: Joseph Meets His Brothers 31
Seminar 16: The Pharaoh Orders Genocide 32
Seminar 17: Moses Kills the Egyptian Overseer 33
Seminar 18: Moses' Obligations 34
Seminar 19: Moses Is Denied Entrance into the Promised Land 35
Seminar 20: The Judges & Temptations 36
Seminar 21: The Story of Ruth 37
Seminar 22: The Selection of David & The Character Quote 38
Seminar 23: Saul's Quote 39
Seminar 24: Nathan's Parable—Rich Man, Poor Man 40:

Seminar 25: Solomon's Strengths & Weaknesses 41
Seminar 26: Esther 42
List of Ethics, Morality, and Responsibility Questions 45
List of Ethics, Morality and Responsibility Questions by Theme 49
Bibliography 53

BACKGROUND

The Ethics Seminar Guide uses the Socratic technique of asking thoughtful, open-ended questions to promote critical thinking and the sharing of ideas as students formulate a perspective that is true to them. Bible stories are used as the background text for the exploration of contemporary issues. While the Bible is not the world's first book, it is the first printed book and the biggest seller of all time. Many of the stories in the Hebrew Scripture, Tanak, also recorded as the Christian Old Testament part of the Bible, were passed down over hundreds of years by oral tradition, storytelling among villagers of ancient times.

A number of these stories have timeless themes with universal messages that are pertinent even among the non-churchgoing members of our society. As we become an increasingly secular society, some people are curious about the influence of the Bible in our Western culture. The companion book, *Bible Stories for All without the Dogma, A Part of Cultural Literacy*, describes the key Bible stories without the doctrine of denominational religions and serves as the reader for *The Ethics Seminar Guide*.

Ethics

The words, ethics and morals, are typically used interchangeably today by a wide range of sources in referring to good or correct conduct. A few sources (e.g., Dictionary.com and Britannica) ddifferentiate between the two terms. Ethics are usually rules developed by others, such as organizations, to clarify what appropriate behavior is. Examples common among many professions include medical, business, and legal ethics. Morals are developed by individuals to guide their behavior and expectations of others. Religions have often influenced the development of personal morals. Non-religious people have also demonstrated high moral examples.

In *The Ethics Seminar Guide*, we will use the terms ethics and morals interchangeably unless otherwise noted. In addition, we will add the term, responsibility, to the discussion since it is so closely related to ethics and morals. Your sense of ethics, morals, and personal responsibility form your compass, your guide for living.

Audience

This guide was written for use by high schools but is also clearly appropriate for middle school and college students. Actually, the seminar questions are useful for folks of any age. I have included several in my companion book, *Bible Stories for All without the Dogma* and have used them in my adult education classes.

Additional Resources:

*"The Socratic Seminar - teaching practices in the classroom," 4 minutes
https://www.youtube.com/watch?v=RBjZ-4MK1WE&feature=fvwrel

"How to do the Socratic Method – Teach Like This," 3 minutes
https://www.youtube.com/watch?v=_CPLu3qCbSU

"The Socratic Method: What it is and How to Use it in the Classroom."
https://tomprof.stanford.edu/posting/810

R.W. Paul's "Six Types of Socratic Questions."
https://psychology.illinoisstate.edu/aehouse/421/421%20log%20folder/Socratic%20questioning.html

*Highly recommended. Viewed about 50,000 times. Used in my classroom.

INTRODUCTION

The goal of this book is to engage you in a discussion of life issues and for you to develop your own compass, a guide for living. We will use Old Testament stories that have universal meaning for your consideration. You may prepare a portfolio of your reflective thoughts as you initially think about the issues presented and then consider other opinions in forming your own thoughts.

In the introduction to his book, *Walking the Bible,* Bruce Feiler describes Abraham as follows: "Abraham was not originally the man he became. He was not an Israelite; he was not a Jew. He was not even a believer in God – at least initially. He was a traveler." Like Abraham, we are travelers moving to what we will become.

As you tackle the issues presented, I hope that you will develop a meaningful compass to help you become the person you want to be in life. It is not easy, but it can be gratifying.

This seminar guide is based on the book, *Bible Stories for All without the Dogma, A Part of Cultural Literacy* by this author. Its companion, *Teacher Supplement to Bible Stories for All without the Dogma*, is designed for grades 5-9 with its focus on reading comprehension, vocabulary development, essay writing, discussion questions, and assessment quizzes.

Bible Stories Background

Although the Bible is a bound book with one cover and one title, it is not a single, unified book. The Bible is actually a collection of many books. In fact, the word bible comes from the Greek words, ta biblia, which means the books. So, the Bible is like a library. In this case a collection of 66 books written by more than 40 authors (e.g., by kings, poets, farmers, teachers, musicians, and fishermen) in several styles including stories, histories, instructions, letters, proverbs, prophecies, songs, and poems. They range in length from one page (2 John) to one hundred pages (Psalms). The Bible is a book about people and God.

THE SEMINAR PROCESS

A seminar is a form of learning in which people meet in small groups to discuss a particular subject. Everyone is expected to participate in this learning process. The principal aim is to develop further insights to a perspective and to develop additional perspectives. Participants may also develop skills, such as active listening, public speaking, and critical analysis. Seminars include elements of the Socratic method of open-ended, thoughtful questions of a perspective. A seminar is a participatory process exploring many perspectives often leading to a multitude of possibilities. The following practices are suggested for your consideration.

Simple, Traditional Classroom Process
- Assign a reading and a question and request a draft written response.
- Hold a classroom discussion in a structured seminar manner as suggested below or in traditional, open discussion format.
- Have an in-class, final written response with input from classroom perspectives.

Classroom Seminar Circle

The Classroom Seminar Circle incorporates elements of the Socratic Method and the seminar process. The Socratic method asks thoughtful, open-ended questions of a perspective while the seminar process uses those insights and explores additional perspectives. The Classroom Seminar Circle opens with a thoughtful, open-ended question, explores further insights to an initial perspective, and then seeks other perspectives and insights. The Classroom Seminar Circle uses an assigned reading to engage students in careful reading, critical thinking, initial explanatory writing, speaking, active listening, and final writing incorporating other viewpoints. In short, read, think write, speak, listen, and revise.

The teacher and students sit in a circle to discuss the assigned reading, its question, and the written responses. The teacher will start by reviewing the ground rules, reading part of the assigned reading and the question, and then open for discussion. As classroom seminar circles progress, the teacher's role evolves from instructing on the process to moderating as the students taking on the responsibility of facilitating a meaningful discussion.

The Classroom Seminar Circle is a structured discussion.
- Develops a further understanding through the discussion of others' opinions
- Encourages all students to participate

- Promotes multiple insights
- Expects active listening
- Facilitates student-engaged learning and answers

Goal: enhanced ethical/moral reasoning
- Also improved listening, comprehension, critical thinking, speech, and writing.

Student Responsibilities
- Read the assigned passage twice for better understanding
- Note one or more interesting phrases and related questions for class discussion
- Write a short reflection on the assigned question

Seminar Etiquette
- Address each other by name
- Sit preferably in a circle facing each other
- Be courteous.
- Pass if you do not wish to speak
- Address only the question raised by your teacher or the one under current discussion

Seminar Teacher/Moderator Tasks
- Prepare your own clarifying questions in case needed
- Summarize the reading and ask the assigned question
- Occasionally rephrase answers to model active listening and ensure understanding
- Request clarification if needed
- Seek two or three responses to each student's perspective on the reading
- Seek multiple perspectives, preferably at least two or three more perspectives
- Encourage participation by all to a near equal degree
- Take notes on student participation and a sample of their comments
- Evaluate student work (see the following example)

Evaluation
- Short, pre-seminar student reflection on the assigned reading
- On the same paper or digital notebook, a short, final reflection drawing on the pre-seminar reflection and the class discussion and noting the new points taken into consideration and the revised concluding opinion
- Student/teacher evaluation of class participation

Frequency

Select appropriate questions from the seminar question list that fit well with your group. Avoid overdoing related questions for additional insights. Consider holding weekly or biweekly seminar sessions. Consider doing whole class seminar evaluations every three to four weeks.

Suggested Process
- Students will ideally sit in a circle with their teacher.
- Seminar discussions work better in small groups enabling all to participate more than once. Recommend groups of 8-12.
    - » Option: Hold the session with the whole class even if larger than twelve. Have students who do not have an opportunity to participate in a circle of 8-12 sit outside the circle, take notes, and share them with an assigned partner who is participating in the discussion. Have the observing students sit in the next seminar circle.
- The teacher will briefly introduce the topic by summarizing the assigned reading and reading the assigned question for discussion. The students are expected to have read the assigned reading and answered the question beforehand.
- Students will respect the speaker. No interrupting. This is not a debate but an active listening session to aid in formulating and revising one's own thoughts. Some teachers consider developing ground rules with their class.
- After announcing the question, the teacher will randomly select a different, volunteering student each session to respond and then proceed around the circle accepting comments on the first student's perspective.
- Students who do not wish to respond at this time may pass but they are expected to participate later in the discussion.
- The teacher will go around the circle several times seeking additional insights to a perspective offered and then additional perspectives and insights to them. End the discussion at a natural conclusion.
- The teacher may repeat a student's statement to ensure everyone understands it or to model active listening.
- In this process of going around the circle, the teacher may ask questions to facilitate the discussion or to clarify a point.
- At the end of the session, the students should write a short, final reflection summarizing their thoughts and the impact of others' thinking.
- Take time to do a student evaluation.
- At the conclusion of the first few sessions, the teacher may want to do a whole class sem-

inar evaluation to help students internalize the expectations and adjust their behavior and participation as appropriate.

Example of Ground Rules
- Be prepared. (Read the assigned reading twice. List 1-2 questions or passages for discussion.)
- Respect the speaker. (Do not interrupt the speaker. This is not a debate. Raise your hand to speak next.)
- Participate in a meaningful way. (Be thoughtful of others.)
- Respect the group by keeping your comments brief and to the point. (Be on task. Think beforehand how you want to focus attention on your key point and keep elaboration concise.)
- Affirm each other's points of view and note your own contribution. (You do this by noting where you are in agreement and adding an additional supporting comment or appreciating another's point of view but politely noting a different perspective. Support your response with examples, if appropriate.)
- Explore, learn new insights, and develop your own thoughts on the issue at hand.

Teacher/Moderator Challenges

While this may appear to be an easy role with little to do, the opposite is actually the case. The teacher's role should evolve from a leader who directs to a moderator who facilitates, observes, and occasionally makes or asks clarifying statements. The moderator must be prepared with key, additional questions that may be needed if they do not arise out of the student discussions. The moderator needs to recognize that not all students will feel comfortable in publicly voicing an opinion. Some students may view a few students as the class experts and may not listen attentively to the others. The moderator needs to work the class so that all voices are heard, and none dominates.

A virtual seminar circle offers its own unique advantages and organizing considerations. At a time when students are socially isolated, a virtual seminar circle requires students to interact in a deliberately thoughtful manner with each other, including fellow students they might not normally interact with. However, some of the techniques that are suitable for a classroom need tweaking for a virtual setting.

Calling on students in alphabetical order is too rote. You could end up calling on students who want to observe while delaying the enthusiastic student with something to share.

You could use the order in which students appear on your screen but that has the same disadvantages of using alphabetical order. In addition, the order on the screen may jump around after students speak.

The use of the chat box to post student interest in speaking is another option. However, the chat box may become unwieldly after a number of posts. It is difficult to monitor the students' screens, their discussions and the chat box simultaneously. Plus, there is the temptation for impatient students to post an actual comment or perspective and thus enable a parallel discussion to develop and perhaps evolve into a debate.

The use of the raised hand icon can facilitate a more orderly and productive discussion. I would encourage the moderator to place a check mark on her/his own paper list of students as each student speaks to ensure no student dominates or is left out of the discussion.

My own preference is a variation in which students indicate their interest in commenting or offering a new perspective by raising their hand so we can all see their interest in speaking. By seeing the students, I can also watch their moods and the intensity of their feelings and make quick, passing comments as the moderator to acknowledge individuals while balancing the group's needs and the process. I would also place a check mark on a paper list of students as each student speaks.

THE REAL WORLD

Why Do Unethical/Immoral Issues Arise?

People sometimes act unethically/immorally. It is thought that we all do at some time. We are human and prone to weak moments. We are especially prone to pressure to act in ways that range from somewhat uncomfortable to downright illegal and repulsive.

On-the-Spot Decision Making

It is hard sometimes when you are put on the spot to make a difficult decision without the time to think it through. How can you align your actions with your values when pressed for an immediate decision without time to think through its ramifications?

I often recall an early lesson I learned in my first career, decades ago, as a manager of a large workforce. A wise senior manager told me, "Don't put anything in writing that you would not want your mother to see." In other words, don't do anything you would not want your mother to know. That advice has stood the test of time for me and many others. Another approach is to think if you would do it to your family or friends. You might consider how you would feel if it was done to you. In addition to these personal considerations, think about the long term. How will your decision be remembered after the heat of the moment? Lastly, think about your heart. That is, how does this decision line up with your character? Who you really are.

How to Handle Situations

When you are in the presence of others in a difficult situation, the first but often tough suggestion in the heat of the moment is to act respectfully. Pause. Use tact. Reach down deep into your soul for the strength you may need. When possible, steer the conversation in a more productive direction before that oncoming, unethical/immoral decision can get voice. Regardless, hang in there and work through the conflict. Set an example. You may not always prevail but hopefully you will plant some seeds that will enable others to grow.

SOCRATES

Who is Socrates, the philosopher whose Socratic Method has had an influence on seminars? He was the son of a stonemason and a midwife, born in 470 BCE. As an adult he lived through the Golden Age of Athens about 449-431 BCE and during the ensuing decades of challenges and decline. He died in 399 BCE.

Since he was not from a noble family, he probably received a basic Athenian education and learned his father's craft. As required of all Athenian men, he served as a citizen soldier. He fought bravely in three battles at Delium, Amphipolis and Potidaea against Sparta and its allied city-states in what was known as the Peloponnesian War.

He married Xanthippe and had three sons. There is little direct evidence about Socrates, but the accounts of others imply he may have earned a living as a stonemason. However, later in life as he began his activities as a "teacher" and philosopher, he appeared to have had little means of supporting himself and his family. While other teachers and philosophers charged money, Socrates proudly refused. While others thought of him as a teacher, he claimed he was not. He said simply that he asked questions seeking the truth.

His critics considered him to be ugly with a snub nose, bulging eyes, and a short, stocky build. Socrates was unlike other philosophers who charged for their training and dressed well. He wore tattered clothes and walked barefooted. And he did not travel to other cities as other thinkers did pursuing intellectual interests.

He is renowned for his contributions to philosophy, especially its ethics branch. He believed that ethics should be based on reason and not the prevailing theology. In this battle of ideas, he challenged many dearly held beliefs at a time when the Golden Age of Athens was fading and many yearned for the good, old days.

Socrates was critical of Athens' democratic and later tyrannical forms of government. His persistent questioning of their leaders often made them look foolish as he pointed out the inconsistencies in their answers. While he had many followers and friends, he also made many enemies. He was an outlier in his political and religious beliefs, his appearance, and his method of leading discussions.

While his enemies could not charge him with a crime for speaking against the state, they were able to levy a religious charge which could be processed under the system of Athenian justice. Religion was part of the state; its obligations were considered civic duties necessary for the survival of all. A religious crime was an offense against the gods and the city of Athens. He was charged with religious impiety for his unorthodox practices of serving the gods by questioning others and receiving guidance directly from the gods. He did not follow the traditional forms of piety by serving the gods with prayers and sacrifices and obtaining interpretations of the gods only from the priests. Furthermore, he was charged with corrupting the youth with his teachings. However, Socrates vehemently denied teaching anyone. He only asked questions and proudly claimed that he had no wisdom.

Socrates was convicted by a jury and sentenced to death at age 70 by drinking a mixture containing a poison, probably hemlock.

STUDENT'S SEMINAR EVALUATION

Student Name: _____   Date: _____

Please rate your efforts as follows:

Outstanding	Good	Satisfactory	Needs Improvement
4	3	2	1

                                                         Student Rating: Teacher Rating:

1. Discussion contributions   _____   _____
2. Active, courteous listening   _____   _____
3. Maintaining focus   _____   _____
4. Thoughtfulness of my pre-seminar reflection   _____   _____
5. Including new information in my final reflection _____   _____

Student Comments:

_____

_____

_____

Teacher Comments:

_____

_____

_____

STUDENTS' WHOLE CLASS SEMINAR EVALUATION

Please rate your efforts as follows:

Outstanding	Good	Satisfactory	Needs Improvement
4	3	2	1

Student Rating:

1. Meaningful, student discussion contributions _____
2. Active, courteous listening displayed _____
3. Nearly equal, engaged participation _____

Student Comments:

_____

_____

_____

_____

THE MAIN PARTS OF THE BIBLE

The Bible is divided into two parts: The Old Testament and the New Testament. The word, testament, means covenant or a solemn agreement between two parties. In the case of the Bible, the covenant is a solemn agreement between God and her/his people with mutual obligations. The obligations imply a strong love for each other. And to many, love is the central force in life.

The Old Testament
The Old Testament is the story of the Israelites (also called the Jews or the Hebrew people) during the time before Jesus and the story of their unique faith in one God. For example, the Book of Genesis describes the creation of the world and the early Israelite leaders (Abraham, Isaac, and Jacob) and also Joseph. The Book of Exodus explains how Moses led the Israelites out of slavery in Egypt and received the Ten Commandments. Later books describe their settlement in the Promised Land, the Kingdom of Israel, their exile, and their return to Israel. The Old Testament is known as the Holy Scripture or Tanak to the Jewish people. Much of the Tanak/Old Testament looked forward to the coming of the Messiah (the hoped-for person who would lead the Israelites who had been conquered by other nations).

The Old Testament stories were passed down by oral tradition until they were finally recorded in writing as late as 800 years later. By comparison the New Testament was recorded within 50 years after the events described.

The New Testament
The New Testament tells the story of Jesus, the early Christians, their new faith in one God, and salvation through Jesus. In other words, it is about a new covenant.

SEMINAR 1. ADAM AND EVE

Reading: *Bible Stories for All without the Dogma, A Part of Cultural Literacy,* Ch. 8, p. 32-35. And/or the Bible, Genesis 2:7-3:24.

Overview: God created Adam and placed him in the lush Garden of Eden. God told Adam, "You may eat the fruit of any tree in the garden, except the tree that gives knowledge of what is good and what is bad. You must not eat the fruit of that tree; if you do, you will die the same day." (Genesis 2:16-17) (Good News Translation, GNT) God then created Eve. A snake in the garden convinced Eve to eat the fruit of the forbidden tree so she would be knowledgeable like God. She convinced Adam to eat the fruit. Perhaps they were curious. Perhaps God was testing them.

Question 1: What is your responsibility (or extent of your loyalty) to those who have helped you?

Optional Question 2: Are there times you should not go along with others? How do you decide? In other words, in today's world of day-to-day interactions, what are the limits to your loyalty?

_____

_____

_____

_____

_____

_____

_____

_____

_____

_____

_____

_____

_____

_____

SEMINAR 2: CAIN AND ABEL

Reading: *Bible Stories for All,* Ch. 9, p. 36-40. And/or Genesis 4:1-15.

Overview: Two brothers, Cain, a farmer, and Abel, a shepherd, offered God a gift of crops and a lamb respectively. God accepted Abel's gift but rejected Cain's. In anger, Cain turned on his brother and killed him. When God asked Cain where his brother was, Cain replied, "I do not know. Am I supposed to take care of my brother?" (Genesis 4:9) (GNT)

Question 3: Am I my brother's keeper? This statement raises the question: what is our responsibility to care for others (e.g., family, friends, neighbors, strangers)?

Optional Question 4: How do you handle anger and rejection while maintaining your sense of morals and responsibility to others?

SEMINAR 3: NOAH

Reading: *Bible Stories for All*, Ch. 10, p. 41-46. And/or Genesis 6:1-8:22.

Overview: Noah, his wife, his three sons, and their wives - four couples - were saved from the flood by building and fleeing in an ark. Let's move the story to contemporary times, such as a huge recession in the economy or a widespread health pandemic causing a spike in unemployment, hunger, homelessness, and serious health problems. Assume that you are blessed with good health, steady employment, and no loss in income. Building on the previous Cain & Abel seminar, let's further explore your personal thoughts on taking care of yourself (as Noah and his family did) and taking care of your community.

Question 5: Self-preservation is critical as a first priority in order to care for others. How far do you go in taking care of yourself? How do you balance the competing individual needs and community needs? How much collective care do you want to provide through your individual actions and those of your church, community, and government (and paid for with your donations and taxes)?

_____

_____

_____

_____

_____

_____

_____

_____

_____

_____

_____

_____

_____

SEMINAR 4: ABRAHAM & EGYPT

Reading: *Bible Stories for All*, Ch. 12, p. 51-54. And/or Genesis 12:10-20.

Overview: Due to a severe famine, Abram and his wife, Sarai, (later in the story their names are changed to Abraham and Sarah) move from Canaan to the delta region of Egypt where pastureland was more fertile for their flocks to graze. However, Abram was concerned about crossing into Egypt. He said to his wife, Sarai, "You are a beautiful woman. When the Egyptians see you, they will assume that you are my wife, and so they will kill me and let you live. Tell them you are my sister; then because of you they will let me live." (Genesis 12:11-12) (GNT)

Question 6: Was Abram morally correct in asking his wife to lie? How do you decide such matters? Under what types of circumstances?

SEMINAR 5: ABRAHAM & THE TRAVELERS

Reading: *Bible Stories for All,* Ch. 13, p. 60-61. And/or Genesis 18:1-8.

Overview: Abraham (their names have now been changed by God to Abraham and Sarah) was now back in Canaan after being kicked out for lying to the Pharaoh about Sarah. Canaan was a sparsely populated, semi-dry area with a few small villages. Long distance travelers moved by foot to their destinations. If they were wealthy enough to own a donkey, they did not ride on it. Donkeys were used to haul supplies tied to them. Travelers were dependent on the hospitality of strangers living along the way between widely spaced villages. Such hospitality was widely practiced among ancient people.

Three travelers were walking by Abraham's tent during the hottest part of the day. He immediately jumped up, greeted them, and offered them food, water, and shelter (i.e., shade) from the sun to give them strength for their journey.

Question 7: What responsibility do you have to care for strangers?

Optional Question 8: How do you see your responsibility fitting into the web of support provided today by your government agencies (international, national, state, and local), NGOs (non-governmental agencies, such as CARE, the International Rescue Committee, etc.), churches/synagogues/mosques/temples, community organizations, and other individual efforts?

_____

_____

_____

_____

_____

_____

_____

_____

_____

_____

_____

SEMINAR 6: ABRAHAM, HAGAR, & ISHMAEL

Background: *Bible Stories for All*, Ch. 13, p. 61-64. And/or Genesis 21:9-21.

Overview: Abraham and Sarah did not have children. In accordance with one of the customs of the time for such situations, Sarah told Abraham to take her slave, Hagar, as a concubine and have a child by her. Abraham and Hagar then had a son, Ishmael. However, Sarah finally had a son, named Isaac, as promised by God. So, Sarah told Abraham to send Hagar and Ishmael away so Ishmael would not inherit Abraham's wealth. Although Abraham was troubled by Sarah's request to send his first-born son away, he did so after consulting with God. He sent them away with some food and water.

Question 9: Let's overlook the consultation with God. Was Abraham's decision to send his concubine and son away morally correct? We are using morals in terms of conscience, one's personal sense of right and wrong.

Optional Question 10: Let's move to modern times. Couples with children split up for a variety of reasons, such as financial, incompatibility, better prospective mates, etc. What is each parent's responsibility for their children?

SEMINAR 7: ABRAHAM & ISAAC

Reading: *Bible Stories for All,* Ch. 14, p. 65-67. And/or Genesis 22:1-19.

Overview: God tested Abraham by directing him to take his son, Isaac, to a mountain in Moriah and offer him as a sacrifice to God. Just as Abraham picked up a knife to kill Isaac, an angel told Abraham not to hurt the boy. God now knew that Abraham will honor and obey God. Some scholars think that this story, which was written about 800 years after the event, may have been first told and then written to distinguish the Israelites from the polytheistic people of the area who occasionally made human sacrifices to please their gods, especially during severe times, such as multi-year droughts. The Israelites' monotheistic God would not require human sacrifice.

Question 11: How do you decide where to draw the line for your responsibilities to leaders, rulers, and bosses who request a questionable action by you, perhaps testing you?

SEMINAR 8: JACOB & ESAU – SIBLING RIVALRY

Reading: *Bible Stories for All,* Ch. 16, p. 71-72. And/or Genesis 25:19-34.

Overview: Abraham's son, Isaac, and his wife, Rebecca, had twins. Esau was born first, and then immediately after him, Jacob. According to the custom of the time, the first-born son, Esau, was entitled to a double share of the inheritance as his birthright.

One day while Jacob was cooking some hearty lentil soup, Esau came home tired and hungry after a long day hunting. He told Jacob to give him some soup. However, Jacob saw an opportunity and agreed providing Esau gave Jacob his birthrights. Esau, who felt like death from his exhaustion and hunger readily agreed, noting what good are birthrights if I do not soon get something to eat.

Question 12: Was Jacob morally correct?

Optional Question 13: What are your personal limitations in taking advantage of a situation where you have the upper hand? What moral principles do you consider?

SEMINAR 9: JACOB'S DECEPTION OF HIS FATHER, ISAAC

Reading: *Bible Stories for All*, Ch. 16, p. 72-74. And/or Genesis 27:1-42.

Overview: While Jacob obtained Esau's birthright, he still needed his father's blessing to seal the transaction. When Isaac was old, blind, and nearing death, he asked Esau to hunt and kill a wild animal and then cook it the way he liked. He told Esau that he would then give Esau his final blessing. Meanwhile, Rebecca overheard them and called for Jacob. They plotted to steal Isaac's final blessing! She instructed Jacob to select two young, fat goats from their flock so she could cook them as Isaac liked. Then Jacob took it to Isaac while pretending to be Esau and received Isaac's final blessing.

Question 14: Is the deception used here an appropriate way to deal with the inheritance inequities of the time which left Esau a double share of the inheritance because he was the first-born son? If not, how would you resolve this issue if it occurred today? Could there be other factors to consider?

SEMINAR 10: LABAN DECEIVES JACOB!

Reading: *Bible Stories for All,* Ch. 17, p. 75-76. And/or Genesis 29:1-30.

Overview: After Jacob stole Isaac's blessing, Esau threatened to kill Jacob who then fled to Abraham's homeland, Haran, where he had relatives. There Jacob met Rachel, fell in love, and proposed marriage. It was customary for the groom to offer the bride's parents a substantial gift to obtain their permission. In some cultures, the parents held the gift in case the marriage failed. However, Jacob arrived in Haran with nothing. He agreed to work for Rachel's father, Laban, for seven years in order to marry Rachel. Laban agreed. On the wedding night, Laban substituted his heavily veiled, oldest daughter, Leah, for Rachel. You can imagine how furious Jacob was when he pulled back his new bride's veil and discovered he had just married the wrong daughter!

When confronted, Laban explained that it was customary to give the oldest daughter in marriage first. He told Jacob that he could also marry Rachel in exchange for another seven years of hard work. Jacob loved Rachel so much that he agreed. Within a few weeks he had a second wife, Rachel, but also an obligation to work seven more years for Laban.

Question 15: Do two wrongs make a right? Jacob had taken advantage of the starving Esau to request his birthright, a double inheritance, and then outrightly deceived his father Isaac, to obtain the blessing needed to seal the transaction. Then Laban took advantage of Jacob's ignorance of local custom to marry off his oldest daughter in place of Jacob's intended bride.

Optional Question 16: What is your obligation to disclose? Some states have laws requiring the disclosure of known defects and damage to homes and cars, such as flood damage, before completing the sale. What is your obligation to disclose known defects?

_____

_____

_____

_____

_____

_____

_____

Additional Comments next page:

SEMINAR 11: JACOB & ESAU RECONCILIATION

Reading: *Bible Stories for All,* Ch. 17, p. 76-79. And/or Genesis 32:3 – 33:4.

Overview: After another six years of working for Laban in exchange for part of his flock, Jacob decided that it was now time to return to his homeland that he had left some 20 years ago. As Jacob approached his homeland, he worried about his brother, Esau, and how he had treated him in trading for the birthright and stealing his father's blessing and how Esau said he would kill Jacob. Jacob wanted to reconcile with his brother. He sent messengers ahead to tell Esau that he was coming as his obedient servant and sent gifts to him. The messengers reported that Esau was on his way with 400 hundred men. Jacob was frightened. As Jacob saw Esau and his 400 men approaching, Jacob ran ahead and bowed down to the ground seven times in front of Esau. "But Esau ran to meet him, threw his hands around him, and kissed him. They were both crying." (Genesis 33:4) (GNT) And so peace was restored between the brothers. Jacob returned to his homeland safely.

Question 17: Do you have a moral obligation to reconcile wrongs you have caused or been a part of? What approaches would you consider?

SEMINAR 12: JOSEPH, THE FAVORITE SON & ANNOYING BROTHER

Reading: *Bible Stories for All*, Ch. 18, p. 80-84. And/or Genesis 37.

Overview: Joseph was the favorite of Jacob's twelve sons, the first son of Jacob's true love, his wife, Rachel. Jacob gave Joseph a beautiful, fine, long robe with sleeves when most shepherds wore coarse, short sleeve tunics. Joseph would give his father bad reports on his brothers' doings when they were away from home tending to the family's flock of sheep and goats. He also dreamt and told his brothers that they would one day bow down before him! The annoyed brothers subsequently kidnapped Joseph and sold him into slavery in Egypt.

Question 18: How do you deal with a difficult relative in a morally appropriate way?

SEMINAR 13: JOSEPH IS ENSLAVED AND THEN UNFAIRLY IMPRISONED

Reading: *Bible Stories for All,* Ch. 19, p. 85-86. And/or Genesis 39.

Overview: Joseph was sold into slavery to a caravan of traders by his brothers, transported to Egypt, and sold to Potiphar, the captain of the Pharaoh's palace guard. Because Joseph worked hard and successfully handled the tasks assigned, Potiphar made him his personal servant and placed him in charge of his household. Then Potiphar's wife falsely accused Joseph of trying to rape her. Potiphar had Joseph imprisoned.

Question 19: How do you handle hopeless, unfair situations over which you have no control?

SEMINAR 14: JOSEPH GIVES GOD CREDIT FOR HIS ABILITY TO INTERPRET DREAMS

Reading: *Bible Stories for All,* Ch. 20, p. 87-88. And/or Genesis 40-41.

Overview: The Pharaoh's wine steward and chief baker had offended the Pharaoh and were imprisoned with Joseph. They each had disturbing dreams that they did not understand. Dreams held a prominent place in ancient times. They believed that the gods used dreams to predict the future. They asked for Joseph's help. He noted that it is God who gives people the ability to interpret dreams. Joseph then went on to interpret the dreams as a prediction that the wine steward would soon be released but the chief baker would be executed. Later when the Pharaoh had a disturbing dream he did not understand, the restored wine steward recommended Joseph to interpret the meaning of the dream. Again, Joseph noted that it is God who gives people the ability to interpret dreams. He went on to correctly predict that Egypt would soon have seven years of plentiful harvests followed by seven years of famine.

Question 20: Do you have an obligation, perhaps out of politeness or moral or ethical duty, to give credit for others' insights and efforts?

SEMINAR 15: JOSEPH MEETS HIS BROTHERS

Reading: *Bible Stories for All,* Ch. 22, p. 95-98. And/or Genesis 44-45.

Overview: During a severe, multi-year famine that gripped the Ancient Near East, Jacob sent his sons to Egypt to buy grain because they were short of food. Upon arrival the brothers were met by Joseph who was now the governor of Egypt, second in command after the Pharaoh and running the day-to-day affairs of the kingdom.

Question 21: How would you react if you were Joseph?

Optional Question 22: If you have not already done so, think on a longer-term basis, how you want the reacquainted family to evolve over time. Do you feel a moral obligation to reconcile?

Optional Question 23: There's an old guerilla war maxim: In every advantage there is a disadvantage. In every disadvantage there is an advantage. How do you see this playing out in Joseph's response? Have you noticed any similar ethical or moral situations today?

SEMINAR 16: THE PHARAOH ORDERS GENOCIDE

Reading: *Bible Stories for All*, Ch. 25, p. 105-106. And/or Exodus 1.

Overview: Joseph's brothers reconciled. They and their families settled in Egypt where they prospered over the next 400 years. A new Pharaoh came to power who did not know how Joseph saved Egypt from the famine hundreds of years ago. He worried that the numerous Israelites might join an enemy if Egypt was attacked. First, he enslaved them to keep them from increasing in number. When that was unsuccessful, he ordered the Egyptian midwives to kill all the newborn Israelite boys to keep them from reproducing. When they failed to do so, he ordered all his subjects to throw every newborn Israelite boy into the Nile.

Question 24: We often face day-to-day questions of moral obligation that compel us to act, even in the face of unpleasantries and other costs. What was a situation that you faced that caused you to look into your soul for the strength to meet a moral obligation?

Optional Question 25: Over the past one hundred years and up to today, the world has experienced dozens of acts of genocide. Describe one example and its unethical and immoral character.

SEMINAR 17: MOSES KILLS THE EGYPTIAN OVERSEER

Reading: *Bible Stories for All,* Ch. 25, p. 106-107. And/or Exodus 2:11-16.

Overview: One day Moses saw an Egyptian overseer kill an enslaved Israelite. He looked around, saw no one watching, and killed the Egyptian.

Question 26: Was Moses right in killing the Egyptian overseer? Do two wrongs make a right in this case?

SEMINAR 18: MOSES' OBLIGATIONS

Reading: *Bible Stories for All,* Ch. 26, p. 113-119. And/or Exodus 4-11.

Overview: After receiving God's instructions to tell the Pharaoh to let the enslaved Israelites go, Moses repeatedly begs off, complaining that he is nobody, that the Israelites will not listen to him, and that he is a poor speaker. Yet he does confront the Pharaoh ten times.

Question 27: Where do you find the strength to fulfill your moral obligations?

SEMINAR 19: MOSES IS DENIED ENTRANCE INTO THE PROMISED LAND

Reading: *Bible Stories for All,* Ch. 27, p. 123-124. And/or Numbers 20:1-13.

Overview: After years of wandering around the Sinai desert, the Israelites were complaining again about the lack of water. God instructed Moses to strike a rock with his stick and water would gush forth. He did, and water gushed forth. However, God reprimanded him for not acknowledging God's role in providing the needed water. As a result, Moses was told that he would not lead the Israelites into the Promised Land. Moses did see the Promised Land from Mt. Nebo in Moab where he subsequentially died. His faithful follower and successor, Joshua led the Israelites into the Promised Land.

Question 28: Was God fair in denying Moses the entrance into the Promised Land? How do you handle disappointing situations?

SEMINAR 20: THE JUDGES & TEMPTATIONS

Reading: *Bible Stories for All,* Ch. 29, p. 132-138. And/or Judges 4, 6-8, 16.

Overview: After Joshua, the Israelites were occasionally led by a series of temporary leaders, called judges. The Israelites would be tempted by the practices of their polytheistic neighbors and fall away from their monotheistic faith. God would punish them with military defeats and the loss of their independence. The Israelites would repent and ask for God's forgiveness. God would forgive them and appoint a judge to temporarily lead the Israelites militarily and religiously. This cycle of the Israelites would then repeat itself after the judge left.

Question 29: Just as the Israelites drifted away from their beliefs and obligations, this happens to many today. What process might you develop to establish your beliefs and your obligations? What process might you develop to re-examine them, amend and/or re-confirm them to fulfill your sense of responsibility?

SEMINAR 21: THE STORY OF RUTH

Reading: *Bible Stories for All*, Ch. 30, p. 139-142. And/or Ruth 1-4.

Overview: The story of Ruth is a story of deep commitment of caring for elders, even those related by marriage who are from a different group of people.

Question 30: What are your responsibilities within your extended family? To what extent? What limitations are there? How does the story of Ruth challenge you?

Note the quote by Ruth to her mother-in-law, Naomi: "Wherever you go, I will go. Wherever you live, I will live. Your people will be my people. And your God will be my God." (Ruth 1:16) (GNT)

SEMINAR 22: THE SELECTION OF DAVID & THE CHARACTER QUOTE

Reading: *Bible Stories for All*, Ch. 32, p. 150-153. And/or 1 Samuel 16:1-13.

Overview: God lost confidence in the first king of the Israelites, Saul. Twice he failed to exactly follow instructions, using his own judgment at a difficult time. So, God had his prophet, Samuel, meet Jesse to select one of his sons to be the next king after Saul's death. As Samuel met each of the sons, he thought this must be the one. However, God said, "Pay no attention to how tall and handsome he is, because I do not judge as people judge. They look at the outward appearance, but I look at the heart." (1Samuel 16:7) (GNT) Subsequently, Samuel asked Jesse if he had any other sons. He had one more, David, the youngest son who was out in the fields tending to their flock. God told Samuel to anoint David. And he did. This decision was not publicly announced. Saul was permitted to continue to rule.

Question 31: How do you judge a person's heart/character? What characteristics are important in leading an ethical and moral life?

_____
_____
_____
_____
_____
_____
_____
_____
_____
_____
_____
_____
_____

SEMINAR 23: SAUL'S QUOTE

Reading: *Bible Stories for All,* Ch. 33, p. 156-160. And/or 1 Samuel 24.

Overview: Saul realized that he had lost God's confidence and that he had become jealous of David's successes. He thought David would succeed him. Saul sought to kill him and began hunting for him. David coincidentally found Saul in a cave taking a break napping, but he did not kill him out of respect to God who had selected Saul as the first king of the Israelites. When Saul awoke and realized David could have killed him, he cried, "You are right, and I am wrong. You have been so good to me, while I have done such wrong to you! ...How often does someone catch an enemy and then let them go unharmed?" (1Samuel 24:17-19) (GNT)

Question 32: Have you been in an ethical or moral situation and had the courage to act as Saul did? Please explain the key facts and your feelings.

SEMINAR 24: NATHAN'S PARABLE—RICH MAN, POOR MAN

Reading: *Bible Stories for All,* Ch. 34, p. 163-164. And/or 2 Samuel 11:1-12:15.

Overview: King David had an affair with Bathsheba, the wife of an officer in his army who was away in battle. When she became pregnant, David ordered the officer to the center of the battle line where he would most likely be killed. And he was. Subsequently, David married Bathsheba. However, God was not pleased and sent his prophet, Nathan, to see David.

Nathan told him a parable (a short story with a moral lesson) of a rich man and a poor man. While the rich man had many cattle and sheep, the poor man had only one lamb which had grown up with his children. The lamb was like a member of the family. One day a visitor came to the rich man's house. The rich man needed to provide hospitality but did not want to kill one of his own animals to prepare a meal for the visitor. Instead he took the poor man's lamb.

David was angry about the rich man and said he should die and pay four times as much as he took. Nathan, in turn, told David that he was that man when he took Uriah's wife. David immediately repented and said he had sinned against God. Nathan informed him that God forgave him, that he would not die, but, because of his misdeed, his child would die. And so, a week after his birth David's son died.

Question 33: What are some modern-day practices that enable the wealthy to take a morally unfair advantage of those less well off?

_____

_____

_____

_____

_____

_____

_____

_____

_____

_____

SEMINAR 25: SOLOMON'S STRENGTHS & WEAKNESSES

Reading: *Bible Stories for All,* Ch. 36, p. 171-177. And/or 1 Kings 1-11.

Overview: Under King Solomon Israel continued to prosper. The Israelite population increased and became wealthier; the kingdom expanded; and conquered nations paid an annual tribute (tax) to Solomon for limited self-rule. Solomon built a temple to God and wrote numerous proverbs and songs. He was knowledgeable about the plant and animal world. Kings from all over sent staff to consult with him. However, he was tempted by his non-Israelite wives to abandon part of his religion and adopt polytheistic practices. Despite Solomon's unbelievable wealth and success due to God, he was not faithful.

Question 34: What personal or moral obligation do you have to those who have helped you?

SEMINAR 26: ESTHER

Reading: *Bible Stories for All,* Ch. 37, p. 178-184. And/or Esther 1-10.

Overview: While the Israelites were exiled to Persia, the Persian king, Xerxes, fell in love with Esther and made her his queen. However, he did not know she was an Israelite. When the king was tricked into signing a proclamation prosecuting the Israelites, Esther's uncle pushed her to intervene with this famous quote: "Don't imagine that you are safer than any other Jew because you are in the royal palace." (Esther 4:13) (GNT)

Question 35: What issues push you to take more moral responsibility as a member of a group when you could have avoided involvement?

Name: _____   Date: _____

Name: _____ Date: _____

LIST OF ETHICS, MORALITY, AND RESPONSIBILITY QUESTIONS

Question 1: What is your responsibility (or extent of your loyalty) to those who have helped you?

Optional Question 2: Are there times you should not go along with others? How do you decide? In other words, in today's world of day-to-day interactions, what are the limits to your loyalty?

Question 3: Am I my brother's keeper? This statement raises the question: what is our responsibility to care for others (e.g., family, friends, neighbors, strangers)?

Optional Question 4: How do you handle anger and rejection while maintaining your sense of morals and responsibility to others?

Question 5: Self-preservation is critical as a first priority in order to care for others. How far do you go in taking care of yourself? How do you balance the competing individual needs and community needs? How much collective care do you want to provide through your individual actions and those of your church, community, and government (and paid for with your donations and taxes)?

Question 6: Was Abram morally correct in asking his wife to lie? How do you decide such matters? Under what type of circumstance?

Question 7: What responsibility do you have to care for strangers?

Optional Question 8: How do you see your responsibility for fitting into the web of support provided today by your government agencies (international, national, state, and local), NGOs (non-governmental agencies, such as CARE, the International Rescue Committee, etc.), churches/synagogues/mosques/temples, community organizations, and individual efforts?

Question 9: Let's overlook the consultation with God. Was Abraham's decision to send his concubine and son away morally correct? We are using morals in terms of conscience, one's personal sense of right and wrong.

Optional Question 10: Let's move to modern times. Couples with children split up for a variety reasons, such as financial, incompatibility, better prospective mates, etc. What is each parent's responsibility for their children?

Question 11: How do you decide where to draw the line for your responsibilities to leaders, rulers, and bosses who request questionable action by you, perhaps testing you?

Question 12: Was Jacob morally correct?

Optional Question 13: What are your personal limitations in taking advantage of a situation where you have the upper hand? What moral principles do you consider?

Question 14: Is the deception used here an appropriate way to deal with the inheritance inequities of the time which left Esau a double share of the inheritance because he was the first-born son? If not, how would you resolve this issue if it occurred today? Could there be other factors to consider?

Question 15: Do two wrongs make a right? Jacob had taken advantage of starving Esau to request his birthright, a double inheritance and then outrightly deceived his father Isaac, to obtain the blessing needed to seal the transaction. Then Laban took advantage of Jacob's ignorance of local custom to marry off his oldest daughter in place of Jacob's intended bride.

Optional Question 16: What is your obligation to disclose? Some states have laws requiring the disclosure of known defects and damage to homes and cars, such as flood damage, before completing the sale. What is your obligation to disclose known defects?

Question 17: Do you have a moral obligation to reconcile wrongs you have caused or been a part of? What approaches would you consider?

Question 18: How do you deal with a difficult relative in a morally appropriate way?

Question 19: How do you handle hopeless, unfair situations over which you have no control?

Question 20: Do you have an obligation, perhaps out of politeness or moral or ethical obligation, to give credit for others' insights and efforts?

Question 21: How would you react if you were Joseph?

Optional Question 22: If you have not already done so, think on a longer-term basis, how you want the reacquainted family to evolve over time. Do you feel a moral obligation to reconcile?

Optional Question 23: There's an old guerilla war maxim: In every advantage there is a disadvantage. In every disadvantage there is an advantage. How do you see this playing out in Joseph's response? Have you noticed any similar ethical or moral situations today?

Question 24: We often face day-to-day questions of moral obligation that compel us to act, even in the face of unpleasantries and other costs. What was a situation that you faced that caused you to look into your soul for the strength to meet a moral obligation?

Optional Question 25: Over the past one hundred years and up to today, the world has experienced dozens of acts of genocide. Describe one example and its unethical and immoral character.

Question 26: Was Moses right in killing the Egyptian overseer? Do two wrongs make a right in this case?

Question 27: Where do you find the strength to fulfill your moral obligations?

Question 28: Was God fair in denying Moses the entrance into the Promised Land? How do you handle disappointing situations?

Question 29: Just as the Israelites drifted away from their beliefs and obligations, this happens to many today. What process might you develop to establish your beliefs and your obligations? What process might you develop to re-examine them, amend and/or re-confirm them to fulfill your sense of responsibility?

Question 30: What are your responsibilities within your extended family? To what extent? What limitations are there? How does the story of Ruth challenge you?

Question 31: How do you judge a person's heart/character? What characteristics are important in leading an ethical and moral life?

Question 32: Have you been in an ethical or moral situation and had the courage to act as Saul did? Please describe and explain the key facts and your feelings.

Question 33: What are some modern-day practices that enable the wealthy to take a morally unfair advantage of those less well off?

Question 34: What personal or moral obligation do you have to those who have helped you?

Question 35: What issues push you to take more moral responsibility as a member of a group when you could have avoided involvement?

LIST OF ETHICS, MORALITY AND RESPONSIBILITY QUESTIONS BY THEME

Personal Responsibility

Question 1: What is your responsibility (or extent of your loyalty) to those who have helped you?

Optional Question 2: Are there times you should not go along with others? How do you decide? In other words, in today's world of day-to-day interactions, what are the limits to your loyalty?

Question 9: Let's overlook the consultation with God. Was Abraham's decision to send his concubine and son away morally correct? We are using morals in terms of conscience, one's personal sense of right and wrong.

Optional Question 10: Let's move to modern times. Couples with children split up for a variety reasons, such as financial, incompatibility, better prospective mates, etc. What is each parent's responsibility for their children?

Question 11: How do you decide where to draw the line for your responsibilities to leaders, rulers, and bosses who request questionable action by you, perhaps testing you?

Question 34: What personal or moral obligation do you have to those who have helped you?

Question 35: What issues push you to take more moral responsibility as a member of a group when you could have avoided involvement?

Responsibility to Care for Others

Question 3: Am I my brother's keeper? This statement raises the question: what is our responsibility to care for others (e.g., family, friends, neighbors, strangers)?

Question 5: Self-preservation is critical as a first priority in order to care for others. How far do you go in taking care of yourself? How do you balance the competing individual needs and community needs? How much collective care do you want to provide through your individual actions and those of your church, community, and government (and paid for with your donations and taxes)?

Question 7: What responsibility do you have to care for strangers?

Optional Question 8: How do you see your responsibility for fitting into the web of support provided today by your government agencies (international, national, state, and local), NGOs (non-governmental agencies, such as CARE, the International Rescue Committee, etc.), churches/synagogues/mosques/temples, community organizations, and individual efforts?

Question 30: What are your responsibilities within your extended family? To what extent? What limitations are there? How does the story of Ruth challenge you?

Relationship

Optional Question 4: How do you handle anger and rejection while maintaining your sense of morals and responsibility to others?

Question 18: How do you deal with a difficult relative in a morally appropriate way?

Question 19: How do you handle hopeless, unfair situations over which you have no control?

Question 20: Do you have an obligation, perhaps out of politeness or moral or ethical obligation, to give credit for others' insights and efforts?

Question 21: How would you react if you were Joseph?

Optional Question 22: If you have not already done so, think on a longer-term basis how you want the reacquainted family to evolve over time. Do you feel a moral obligation to reconcile?

Optional Question 23: There's an old guerilla war maxim: In every advantage there is a disadvantage. In every disadvantage there is an advantage. How do you see this playing out in Joseph's response? Have you noticed any similar ethical or moral situations today?

Morality

Question 6: Was Abram morally correct in asking his wife to lie? How do you decide such matters? Under what type of circumstance?

Question 12: Was Jacob morally correct?

Optional Question 13: What are your personal limitations in taking advantage of a situation where you have the upper hand? What moral principles do you consider?

Optional Question 25: Over the past one hundred years and up to today, the world has experienced dozens of acts of genocide. Describe one example and its unethical and immoral character.

Question 33: What are some modern-day practices that enable the wealthy to take a morally unfair advantage of those less well off?

Fairness

Question 14: Is the deception used here an appropriate way to deal with the inheritance inequities of the time which left Esau a double share of the inheritance because he was the first-born son? If not, how would you resolve this issue if this occurred today? Could there be other factors to consider?

Question 15: Do two wrongs make a right? Jacob had taken advantage of starving Esau to request his birthright, a double inheritance, and then outrightly deceived his father Isaac, to obtain the blessing needed to seal the transaction. Then Laban took advantage of Jacob's ignorance of local custom to marry off his oldest daughter in place of Jacob's intended bride.

Optional Question 16: What is your obligation to disclose? Some states have laws requiring the disclosure of known defects and damage to homes and cars, such as flood damage, before completing the sale. What is your obligation to disclose known defects?

Question 17: Do you have a moral obligation to reconcile wrongs you have caused or been a part of? What approaches would you consider?

Question 26: Was Moses right in killing the Egyptian overseer? Do two wrongs make a right in this case?

Question 28: Was God fair in denying Moses the entrance into the Promised Land? How do you handle disappointing situations?

Strength of Your Convictions

Question 24: We often face day-to-day questions of moral obligation that compel us to act, even in the face of unpleasantries and other costs. What was a situation that you faced that caused you to look into your soul for the strength to meet a moral obligation?

Question 27: Where do you find the strength to fulfill your moral obligations?

Question 29: Just as the Israelites drifted away from their beliefs and obligations, this happens to many today. What process might you develop to establish your beliefs and your obligations? What process might you develop to re-examine them, amend and/or re-confirm them to fulfill your sense of responsibility?

Question 31: How do you judge a person's heart/character? What characteristics are important in leading an ethical and moral life?

Question 32: Have you been in an ethical or moral situation and had the courage to act as Saul did? Please describe and explain the key facts and your feelings.

BIBLIOGRAPHY

Good News Bible, New York: American Bible Society, 1992.

Caterini, Fran and Gagne, Ellen. "Seminars for Deep Comprehension and Moral Reasoning." Association of Independent Maryland Schools Fall Conference, October 21, 2002, Baltimore, MD.

Feiler, Bruce. *Walking the Bible.* New York: William Marrow, 2001.

Takacs, Stefanie and Barry, Cynthia. "Touchstones Discussion Project Workshop." Association of Independent Maryland Schools Fall Conference, October 31, 2011, Baltimore, MD.

Walsh, Kenneth E., *Bible Stories for All without the Dogma.* Columbia, MD: Summit Crossroads Press, 2020.

"What's the Difference Between 'Morals' and 'Ethics'?" www.dictionary.com/e/moral-vs-ethical Accessed 15 July 2020.

"What's the Difference Between Morality and Ethics?" https://www.britannica.com/story/whats-the-difference-between-morality-and-ethics *.Encyclopædia Britannica*, Cydney Grannan. Accessed July 15, 2020.

"The Socratic Seminar—Teaching Practices in the Classroom." https://www.youtube.com/watch?v=RBjZ-4MK1WE&feature=fvwrel Bill Wesley, Sep 7, 2011. Accessed July 15, 2020.
"Ethics 4 Everyone, A Workshop on Personal Business Ethics, A Leader's Guide." https://www.trainingabc.com/product_files/P/ethics4everyone_lg.pdf. Skill Builders, Inc. Accessed July 17, 2020.

"Ethics 4 Everyone, A Workshop on Personal Business Ethics, A Leader's Guide." https://www.trainingabc.com/product_files/P/ethics4everyone_lg.pdf. Skill Builders, Inc. Accessed July 17, 2020.

If you liked this book,

please add a review

on Amazon.com.

Thank you.

Other books by Kenneth E. Walsh

available at Amazon.com:

and other online retailers:

Bible Stories for All Without the Dogma

and

A Teacher's Supplement to Bible Stories

for All Without the Dogma

www.ingramcontent.com/pod-product-compliance
Lightning Source LLC
Chambersburg PA
CBHW060427010526

44118CB00017B/2396